LOCAL RED BOOKS

C000186866

YORK

DUNNINGTON · HAXBY · TADCASTER

CONTENTS

Redbooks showing the way

Every effort has been made to verify the accuracy of information in this book but the publishers cannot accept responsibility for expense or loss caused by an error or omission.

Information that will be of assistance to the user of the maps will be welcomed.

The representation on these maps of a road, track or path is no evidence of the existence of a right of way.

Street plans prepared and published by ESTATE PUBLICATIONS, Bridewell House, TENTERDEN, KENT. The Publishers acknowledge the co-operation of the local authorities of towns represented in this atlas.

Ordnance Survey® This product includes mapping data licensed from Ordnance Survey® with the permission of the Controller of Her Majesty's Stationery Office.

© Crown Copyright   All rights reserved
© Estate Publications 585-03   ISBN 1 84192 306 0   Licence number 100019031

www.ESTATE-PUBLICATIONS.co.uk

LEGEND

— Motorway
— (road)
— (road)
— Road

══ Pedestrianized / Restricted Access

══ Track

Built Up Area

- - - Footpath

~ Stream

~ River

Lock Canal

—▬— Railway / Station

● Post Office

P / P+ Car Park / Park & Ride

C Public Convenience

+ Place of Worship

→ One-way Street

i Tourist Information Centre

▲8 ▲8 Adjoining Pages

Area Depicting Enlarged Centre

Emergency Services

Industrial Buildings

Leisure Buildings

Education Buildings

Hotels etc.

Retail Buildings

General Buildings

Woodland

Recreation Ground

Cemetery

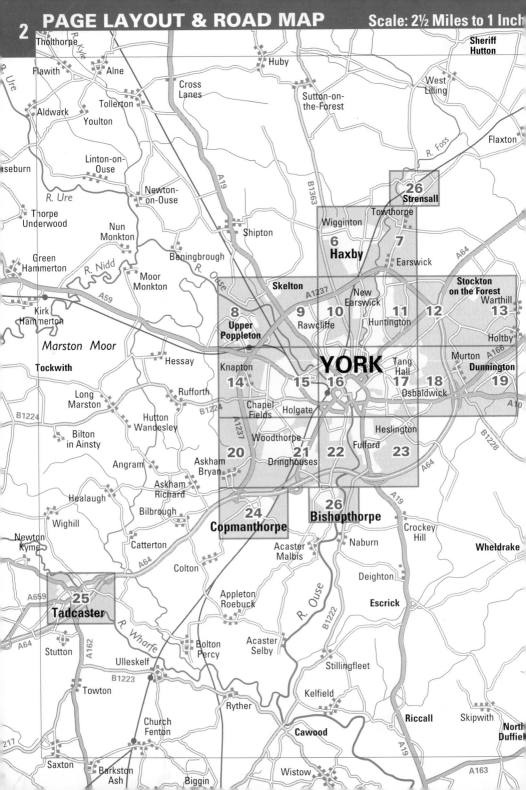

PLACES OF TOURIST & HISTORIC INTEREST

Bar Convent Museum	4 B5	St Georges Field	5 E5
Barbican Centre	5 F6	St Marys Abbey	4 C2
Black Swan Public House	5 F3	St Williams College	5 E2
Bootham Bar Hotel	4 D2	Scarborough Bridge	4 A2
Castle Mill Bridge	5 E5	Skeldergate Bridge	5 E6
Central Library	4 C2	The ARC	
City Screen Cinema	4 D3	(Archaeological Resource Centre)	5 E3
Cliffords Tower	5 E5	Theatre Royal	4 D2
Deans Park	4 D1	Treasurers House	5 E1
Fairfax House	5 E4	Victoria Bar	4 C5
Fishergate Bar	5 F5	Walmgate Bar	5 G5
Fishergate Tower	5 E5	War Memorial Gardens	4 B3
Grand Opera House	4 D4	York Brewery	4 B4
Guildhall	4 D3	York Castle & Museum	5 E5
Jorvik Viking Centre	5 E4	York City Art Gallery	4 C1
Kings Manor	4 C2	York Dungeon	4 D4
Layerthorpe Bridge	5 F2	York Minster	4 D2
Lendal Bridge	4 C3	York Model Railway	4 B4
Lendal Tower	4 C3	York Story Heritage Centre	5 E4
Mansion House	4 C3	Yorkshire Museum	4 C2
Merchant Adventurers Hall	5 E4	Yorvik Brass Rubbing Centre	4 D5
Merchant Taylors Hall	5 E2		
Micklegate Bar & Museum	4 B5	**Medieval Churches**	
Monk Bar	5 E2	All Saints, North St	4 C4
Museum Gardens	4 C2	All Saints, Pavement	5 E4
National Railway Museum	4 A3	Holy Trinity, Goodramgate	5 E2
Newgate Market	5 E3	Holy Trinity, Micklegate	4 C4
Odeon Cinema	4 B5	St Cuthberts	5 F2
Ouse Bridge	4 D4	St Denys	5 F4
Red Tower	5 G4	St Helens	4 D3
Regimental Museum	5 E4	St Martin-le-Grand	4 D3
Richard III Museum	5 E2	St Marys	4 C5
Robin Hoods Tower	4 D1	St Michael le Belfry	4 D2
Roman Bath Inn	4 D3	St Olaves	4 C2
St Anthonys Hall	5 F3		

Tourist Information Centres

York Tourism Board,
20, George Hudson St.   4 C4

City of York Council Services, Guide Friday,
De Grey Rooms, Exhibition Sq.   4 D2
& York Railway Station.   4 B4

Guided Tours of York

River Boat Cruises   4 C3 & 4 D5

Guide Friday operate open top guided bus tours

Haunted City Walks
The Original Ghost Walk,
King's Arms Pub, Ouse Bridge.   4 D4
The Ghost Hunt, Shambles.   5 E3

YORK ENLARGED CENTRE

4

College

E   F   HEWORTH   G   H

16   A1036   GROVE

Glen
Gardens

1

2

17

FOURTH AVENUE

St Williams College

Layerthorpe

EBOR
INDUSTRIAL
ESTATE

Tang Hall Brook

Foss
Islands

3

Merchant Taylors Hall

St Anthonys Hall

The Black Swan P.H

The ARC

Ambulance Station

Navigation
Warehouse

Red
Tower

4

17

YORK
EBVRACVM

Bus
Depot

5

Merchant Adventurers Hall

Foss
Bridge

Walmgate
Bar

Cliffords
Tower

The Eye
of York

York
Castle
Museum

LAWRENCE   STREET

A1079

Georges
Field

Castle
Mills Br

FISHERGATE

Fishergate
Tower

Fishergate
Bar

PARAGON

Barbican
Centre

Swimming
Pool

6

School

School   16   G   H

ROAD

MELBOURNE   ST ANNS CT

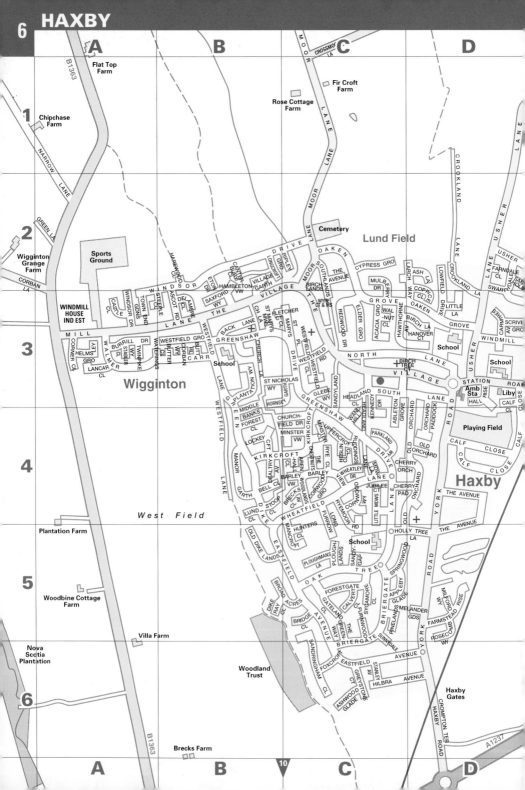

E **F** **G** **H**

Oakbutts Farm

BARLEY RISE
RYEC 26
YORK
BIRCH TREE CL
ST WILFRID
CL CARR LA
BORDER
HOWARD
HOLLIS
CKS
Playground

USHER LANE

Goland Dike

FARRIERS CHASE
WAINGROFT

Strensall Camp

CHESHIRE
AVENUE

Sports Ground

Playing Field

1

ROAD

Towthorpe Bridge

TOWTHORPE

Towthorpe

ALEXANDRA ROAD

Low Farm

STRENSALL

Manor Farm

Willow Farm

STRENSALL PARK

STRENSALL PARK

STRENSALL PARK

Towthorpe Common

Depot

2

Whiteland Field

ARK
DALE ROAD
KELDALE
SWARTHDALE
LANSDOWN WY
MALLARD CL
WOODCOCK CL
FOLKS CL

NEW FORGE CT
OLD COPPICE
CHATSWORTH DR
RIVERSDALE
NETHERWINDINGS

NOOKS
THORNHILLS

WEST GARTHS END

The Nesses

Moat

Grange Farm

ROAD

STRENSALL

ROAD

TOWTHORPE

South Villa Farm

MOOR

LANE

3

River Foss

TOWTHORPE
LINLEY AV
THE LANDINGS

Haxby Landing

Hall Farm

MOOR

LANE

Earswick Grange

LANE

MOOR

LANE

4

Foss Way

LANDING

Sewage Works

LOCKHOUSE LA
LOCKHOUSE WH
WHITELANDS
EARSWICK CHASE

Hall

EARSWICK

CHASE

NORTH AV
SOUTH

WHITELANDS

STRENSALL

WISKER LANE

5

WILLOW GROVE

Earswick

EARSWICK VILLAGE
ROWLEYS CT
STABLERS WK
FIR TREE CL
SHILTON GARTH CL

ROAD

Wisker Farm

6

RIVERSIDE
CRES
ABBOTS WK
GAIT
VESPER WK
MULBERRY CT
KINGSCLERE
CONNAUGHT
STRENSALL ROAD
AVON
CHNAN CT
LERE CT
KN WY
LANG RD
BROOM
DRIVE
TRENT
WITHAM DR
LANGLEY CT
BROOME WY

A1237

11

WISKER LANE

E **F** **G** **H**

A **B** **C** **D**

1
2
3
4
5
6

Overton Grange

New Farm

SHIPTON
A19

CHURCH LANE
ST GILES RD
THE MEADOWS
ST GILES
THE BELL
THE GRN
THE ORCHARD
VIEW
THE VALE
THE GRANGE CL
ROAD

Overton

STRIPE LANE

Folly Bridge

Golf Course

Factory

Fairfield Farm

Church Farm

Moat

Overton Manor

New Farm

Popleton Reach

Skelton Bridge

Ouse Moor

CINDER LANE

Overton Ings

River Ouse

Moat

OUSE MOOR LANE

POPPLETON HALL GDNS

CHURCH LANE

Nether Poppleton

COMMONCROFT LANE

MAIN STREET

RIVERSIDE GDNS

RIVERSALE DR

RIVERSIDE

LITTLEFIELD CL

FERRY LANE

PARK STREET

MILLFIELD

HILLCREST AV

BANKSIDE CL

SPRINGFIELD RD

ALLERTON WY

NETHER WAY

HAWTHORNE CL

WAY

LITTLE GARTH

HUTTON CL

NURSERY ROAD

MILLFIELD GDNS

Sports Ground

Lby

MAIN STREET

DIKE LANE

EBOR CL

NETHER WAY

MONTAGUE WK

EBOR

ELM TREE AV

PEAR TREE AV

WAY

EBOR GARTH

DRIVE

MIDWAY

AV

NURSERY CL

West Field

School

OLD SCHOOL CL

BEECH WY

LIME GARTH

CHANTRY CL

GAP

CHANTRY GROVE

APPLE GARTH

CHERRY GRO

ORCHARD

SYCAMORE AV

FAIRWAY

LONG DR

RIDGE DR

EASTHORPE DR

SANDYRIDGE

LINTON RD

MILLFIELD LANE

Mill Field

WEST FIELD

Upper Poppleton

SCHOOL

MAIN STREET

BRACKENHILLS

DIKELANDS CL

LONG

STATION LANE

LONG RIDGE

Millfield Farm

BEECH GRO

COPPER BEECH CL

WESTFIELD CL LANE

WILLOW CFT

The Green

DIKE LANE

STATION LANE

MANOR CL

MILLFIELD LA

GREAT NOR
KYLE
INGS
CAE
EBOR AV
NIDD WY
WY

MILLFIELD LANE

Grange Farm

HODGSON

Crescent Farm

A59

Motel

A

BLACK DIKE

JACK DIKE LA

B

ROAD

POPPLETON STATION

14

POPPLETON

C

A1237

D

MILLFIELD

BOROUGHBRID

Wor

A   **B**   **C**   **D**

B1363   Brecks Farm   6   A1237

1

Moor Plantation

Haxby Road Farm

School

York Riding School

Playing Field

Park Lodge

A1237

2

Kettlestring Farm

New Earswick

Clifton Moor

WIGGINTON ROAD

School

Rec Grnd

3

STIRLING   AUDAX   ROAD

NORTH YORK TRADING ESTATE

Works

Golf Driving Range

Kettlestring South Farm

Recreation Ground

Rec Grnd

Liby

Playing Field

Swim Pool

STATION AV

Playing Field

4

Playing Field

Bootham Stray

Caravan Site

MEADOW-FIELDS DR

9

5

Depot

TRADING ESTATE

Playing Field

Rugby Football Ground

Works

Bootham Stray Gates

Depot

Warehouse

Factory

Sports Ground

6

Schools

School

Playing Field

Playing Field

Swimming Pool

River Foss

A   **B**   16   **C**   **D**

B1363

WIGGINTON ROAD

Clifton

A B C D

Huntington North Moor

TURBARY LANE

Turbaries

WISKER LANE

ROAD A64

LANE

NORTH LANE

1

Priest's Closes

Caravan Site

MALTON ROAD

Huntington and Stockton Drain

Forest Park Golf Club

STOCKTON HALL HOSPITAL

DE MAUL PL

Stockton on the Forest

A1237

THE VILLAGE

STONE

CHAUMONT WY

THE LIME

2

Club Ho

THE

KINGS MOOR

CHAUMONT WY

MANOR

11

OLD MALTON ROAD

Old Foss Beck

Sewage Works

LANE

Cattle Breeding Centre

KINGS MOOR ROAD

3

HOPGROVE LANE NORTH

Hopgrove Farm

Sow Dike

ROAD

Oaklands Farm

STOCKTON

HOLTBY

HOPGROVE

BRANDON GRO

LANE

4

Stockton On The Forest

WHEELD DR

HOPGROVE LA

SOUTH LANE

MALTON

A1036

Tang Hall Beck

ROAD

11

Westfield Farm

Stockton West Moor

LANE

HOLTBY

Turk

5

ld

Rowe's Cottage Farm

Glebe Farm

STOCKTON LANE

LANE

BARGAIN LANE

Sandfield Farm

PIKER

6

Ivy House Farm

Cow Moor Farm

BARGAIN LANE

BAD

A64

BAD MOOR LANE

THORN LA

Piker Thorn Beck

18

A B C D

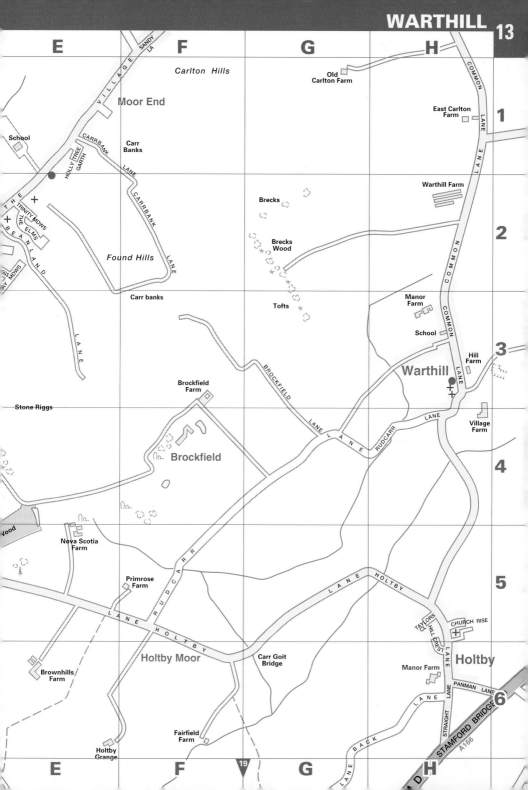

E   F   G   H

Carlton Hills

Old Carlton Farm

Moor End

East Carlton Farm

1

School

Carr Banks

CARRBANK LANE

HOLLY TREE GARTH

Warthill Farm

Brecks

TRINITY MDWS

THE ELMS

BEANLAND

Brecks Wood

2

COMMON LANE

CARRBANK LANE

Found Hills

Tofts

Manor Farm

School

Carr banks

LANE

BROCKFIELD LANE

Warthill

Hill Farm

3

Stone Riggs

Brockfield Farm

LANE

RUDCARR LANE

Village Farm

Brockfield

4

Wood

Nova Scotia Farm

RUDCARR

HOLTBY LANE

Primrose Farm

HOLTBY LANE

5

LANE

RUDCARR

HOLTBY

TAYLORS CL

CHURCH RISE

HILL CREST

Holtby

Brownhills Farm

Holtby Moor

Carr Goit Bridge

Manor Farm

PANMAN LANE

STRAIGHT LANE

STAMFORD BRIDGE

6

A166

Fairfield Farm

Holtby Grange

LANE BACK

E   F   19   G   D   H

A **B** **8** **C** **D**

POPPLETON

Crescent
Farm
A59
Motel
BOROUGHBRIDGE
Red Lion
Bridge

1

Bur Field

ROAD
BOROUGHBRIDGE
ROAD

Sports
Ground

Wheat
Lands

NORTHMINSTER
BUSINESS PARK

Fir Tree
Farm

2

Knapton Moor

NORMAN DRIVE

ALBION

GRAYSHON DR

SHERWOOD

GROVE

AVENUE

BECKFIELD

MELWOOD GRO

Huntsham
Farm

LANE

North Field

School

SUNNINGDALE
CL
TROON
CL

3

MOOR

PRESTWICK
CT

GREENSBOROUGH

BIRKDALE
GRO

MUIRFIELD

DRIVE

VILLAGE

Knapton

BACK

ST PETERS
CL

Ten Thorn
Farm

New House
Farm

STREET

LANE

TURNBERRY

CARNOUSTIE
CL

LOCH
PL

MELANDER
CL

4

LOWFIELD

LANE

TEN

THORN

LANE

KNAPTON LANE

BECKFIELD

Low Field

LOWFIELD LANE

BLAND

BRIAR AV

COLLINGHAM
PL

FELLBROOK AV

RUNSW

B1224

Whinney
fields

WETHERBY

ROAD

WETHERBY

5

Chapel
Fields

FIELDS

ROAD

GROVE

ROAD

MARSTON CR

MARSTON AV

Recreati
Groun

CHAPEL

BRAMHAM

BRANTON
PL

BRIDLE

BRAMHAM

BARKSTON

AVENUE

RYLATT
PL

BARKSTON

HESLEY
PL

BARKSTON
PL

GRO

WALTON

AVENUE

The
Grange

CHAPEL FIELDS

GRO

HOTHAM AV

PARKER
AV

HOTHAM

6

GRANGE

LANE

GRANGE LANE

GRANGE

THE WANDLE

ROAD

BRAMHAM

ASKHAM

School

Wes
Fiel

Bachelo
Hill

RIDGEWAY

A **B** **20** **C** **D**

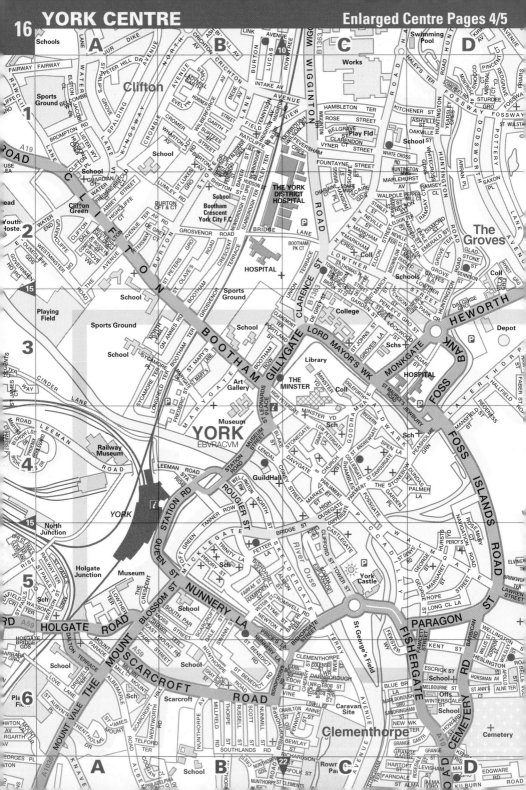

Holtby Grange

Fairfield Farm

13

S A166 STAMFOR

Holtby Manor

Providence Farm

BACK LANE

STAMFORD BRIDGE ROAD

LANE S

1

Osbaldwick Beck

VENGEANCE LANE

Mill Hill

Holtby Manor

BRIDGE ROAD

STAMFORD

CHURCH BALK LANE

Thorntree Field

EASTFIELD

SPRING BNK
AV

CHURCH LANE

THE COPPER BEECHES

CHURCH

THE BEECH DRI

COPPER

MANOR YORK

STOCKHILL CL

GARDEN FLAT LANE

GORSLEY HILL

HOLLY TREE CROFT

HOLLY TREE LA

ASPEN CL

PETERCROFT CL

PETERCROFT LA

KENDAL

LINDENCROFT

HORSFIELD

UNDERCROFT

WEST THORNCROFT

KERVER LANE

SAWYERS WK

KEEPERS LANE

TWIN CT

LANE

2

School

HUNTERS CL

PEARTREE LA

CHURCH LANE

The Manor Beeches

Library

OWLWOOD DERWOOD CFT LA

OWLWOOD LANE

SCH LANE

STREET

COMMON

WATER LANE

WOOD MWS

ELM CL

THORNCROFT MWS

ASHDALE RD

THE GRN

SCAUDER CROFT

CALDER CL

OX WAY CL

3

ROAD

DERWENT LA

PIT LANE

DERWENT EST LANE

Dunnington

CEDAR GLADE

CURLEW GLEBE

GREEN

HUNTERS WOOD

DEERSTONE WY

GREENSIDE WK

GREENSIDE WY

GREENSIDE

GREENSIDE

INTAKE

THE END

Playing Field

Sports Club

3

Thorntree Hill

CEDAR GLADE

Hassacarr Bridge

YORK

Grimston Court

Undergate Field

Sewage Works

Hassacarr Pond

HASSACARR LA

CHESSINGHAM PK

Hall Garth

4

C

Ings Drain

The Plantation

DERWENT VALLEY INDUSTRIAL ESTATE

HAGG LANE

LANE

A1079

5

New Field

Common Drain

CONEYGARTH LANE

LANE

Breckon Farm

COMMON LANE

6

ELVINGTON LANE

B1228

Dunnington Common

Common Farm

E F G H

Column/Row grid: E, F, G, H across; 1, 2, 3, 4, 5, 6 down.

School
Sports Centre
Playing Field
St Stephens
St Stephens Road
Ground
MOORGARTH AV
MOORGARTH
ST GEORGES PL
NEWINGTON CT
GARDENS
PULLEYN
DRIVE
A1036
Holgate Beck
School 15
Micklegate Stray
Hob Moor
Cycle Path
Swimming Pool
Playing Field
Sports Club
Track
Indoor Bowls
HILLCREST GDS
CHALFONTS AV
NELSONS
LANE
NELSON
Commn Cent
FARM
LANDS
School
Sports Ground
School
Liby
Hotel
Hotel
Racing Stables
Dringhouses
Hogg's Pond
HUNTER'S
THE HORSESHOE
THE HORSESHOE
THE COVERT
MIDDLETHORPE
BRACKEN ROAD
Rec Grnd
School
ALDERSYDE
OLD MOOR
ASHFIELD
CT
P+
York College of Art and Technology
Hospice
The Wilberforce Home
Supermarket
P
Burial Ground
Sim Hills
THE GROVE
CHESSINGHAM GDS
College
Playing Field
Knavesm Wood
DRINGTHORPE
Marsh Farm
Nairn Cl
Spey Bank
Annan Cl
Bogs (Nature Reserve)
Hills Golf Course
TADCASTER ROAD
TADCASTER ROAD
Middlethorpe Grange
B A L K
A64
GREEN
SIM
CHURCH
ROAD
24
F
G
26
H
TADCASTER ROAD

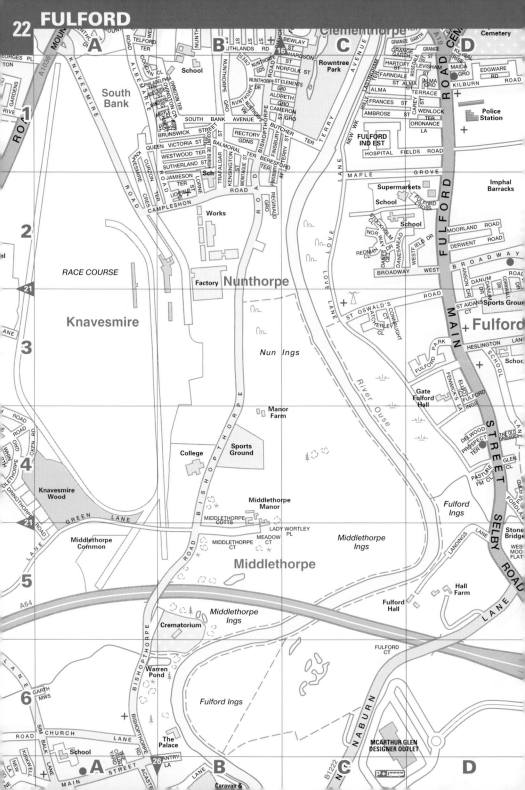

FULFORD

A1036 ROAD

MOUNT

KNAVESMIRE

ROAD

A **B** **C** **D**

Cemetery

GEORGES PL
TON

MINTHORPE DR
TELFORD TER

School

ALBEMARLE ROAD

ST PHILADELPHIA
WINDSOR TER
ADELPHIA TER
DONINGTON CL
LONINGTON CA
ARGYLE ST

South Bank

NUNTHORPE GRO

NORFOLK
ST

CLEMENTHORPE

BEWLAY
RICHARDSON ST

GRANGE GARTH

GRANGE
GRANGE
GARTH
RISE

HARTOFT ST

Rowntree Park

GRANGE GRO

LEVISHAM ST

MAIDA

A19

KILBURN

Police Station

EDGWARE
ROAD

SOUTHLANDS RD

NUNTHORPE DR
NUNTHORPE
GRO

ST CLEMENTS

ALDRETH
GRO

CAMERON
GRO

BUTCHER TER

FARNDALE
ST ALMA

ALMA
TERRACE

ALMA
GRO

CAREY
ST

ST ALMA

FRANCES ST

AMBROSE ST

WENLOCK TER

ORDNANCE
LA

Imphal
Barracks

SOUTH BANK AVENUE

BRUNSWICK STREET

QUEEN VICTORIA ST

WESTWOOD TER

SUTHERLAND ST

JAMIESON TER

LICHFIELD

LORNE

CAMPLESHON

KNAVESMIRE CRES

CURZON TER

KNAVESMIRE ROAD

BALMORAL TER

TRAFALGAR ST

KENSINGTON

MONTAGUE ST

Sch

RECTORY GDNS

BERESFORD TER

REGINALD GRO

FINSBURY AV

BISHOPTHORPE ROAD

TERRY ST

TERRY AV

FULFORD IND EST

HOSPITAL FIELDS ROAD

LANE

MAPLE

GROVE

Supermarkets

School

School

FULFORD CROSS

MOORLAND ROAD

DERWENT ROAD

B R O A D W A Y

ROAD

DANUM DR

CORNWALL
DR

ANSON DR

Sports Ground

2

A1036 ROAD

RACE COURSE

Factory

Works

Nunthorpe

LOVE LANE

STOCKHOLM

REDMAN
CL

NOR WAY
DANES DR
DANESMEAD

WEST FIELD DR

WEST

BROADWAY

ST AIDANS DR

Fulford

21

Knavesmire

Nun Ings

River Ouse

ST OSWALD'S
CATCHERLEY
CT
CL

CONNAUGHT
CT

ROAD

FULFORD PARK

HESLINGTON

School

School

3

BISHOPTHORPE

Manor Farm

College

Sports Ground

Middlethorpe Manor

MIDDLETHORPE COTTS

LADY WORTLEY PL

Gate Fulford Hall

FULFORD
FENWICK'S LA
FULFORD
INGS

ELLIOT

DELWOOD
PROSPECT TER

PASTURE
FM CT

Fulford Ings

The Old Orchard

GLEN CL

4

Knavesmire Wood

DRINGTHORPE ROAD

WHIN

CKEN GRO
ROAD

GREEN LANE

MIDDLETHORPE CT

MEADOW CT

Middlethorpe Ings

LANDINGS
LANE

FORD LA

21

Middlethorpe Common

Middlethorpe

STREET

SELBY ROAD

Stone Bridge

WEST
MOOR
FLAT

5

A64

Middlethorpe Ings

Crematorium

Hall Farm

Fulford Hall

LANE

6

GARTH MWS

SIM

KIRKWELL

BALK LANE

NEW

ROAD

CHURCH LANE

BISHOPTHORPE ROAD

COLTER
YARD

Warren Pond

Fulford Ings

FULFORD CT

NABURN

B1222

P+

MCARTHUR GLEN DESIGNER OUTLET

School

The Palace

GANTRY
LA

MAIN

STREET

ACASTER

26

A **B** **C** **D**

Caravan &

COPMANTHORPE

The Foss

Beckett's Crossing
York Field

Temple Field

Mill Ruddings

TEMPLE GARTH

DROME ROAD

TEMPLE LANE

ROPERS
WHISTLER CT
FLETCHERS
BOWYERS
YORKFIELD WY
LEARMANS WY
WATT CLERS
WAINERS CL
BARBERS DR
HATTERS CL
POTTERS DR
DRAPERS CET
COOPERS DR
WAGGONERS DR
WEAVERS
FARRIERS AN
FLAXMAN AV
SADDLERS CROFT
MILL CROFT
FABER CL
GARDENERS
WHEELWRIGHTS
FARMERS WAY
WYERS CRES
Schools
Sports Ground

MERCHANT WY
MERCHANT LA
MAN HORSEMAN
LARKFIELD CL
ST NICHOLAS CL
LINNET
THE MOUNT
PIKE HILLS
COLLEGE CRES
ST NICHOLAS RD
HALLCROFT RD
HEATH ROAD
MANOR HEATH
LYNWOOD WW
HORSEMAN DR
RUTLAND CL
SCHOOL LA
LYNWOOD AV
Pol Sta
Horseman Lane

Club Ho

Pike Hills Golf Course

MANOR LANE

ASKHAM MILL LANE
ASKHAM FIELDS LA
ASKHAM FLDS LA
LANE

Ebor Way (Roman Road)

Copmanthorpe

GREEN CL
LOW ST
FAIRFAX CROFT
VAVASOUR CT
MALBIS CRES
BELLMANS CT
BARONS CROFT
ST GILES WY
VICARS GARTH
BEADLE GARTH
BARON STREET
DEACONS CT
GILES CT
STATION ROAD
MAIN STREET
HOBSON CL
NALTON CT
SEDLEY CT
DYKES LANE
MOORLAND
STN

LOW
WESTFIELD

BARNFIELD
PADDOCK LA
BACK LANE
HOMEFIELD FM
MANOR FM
WHISTROP FM
ROAD

Cemetery

MOOR

GREEN BALK

WESTFIELD LOW

Low Westfield

Moor Lane Farm

MOOR LANE

GARFIT

TADCASTER

Pike Hills Golf Course

A1237
A64
A20

Askham Bryan College of Agriculture & Horticulture

Westfield House

Ribble Sykes

Hagg Wood

Town Ings Drain

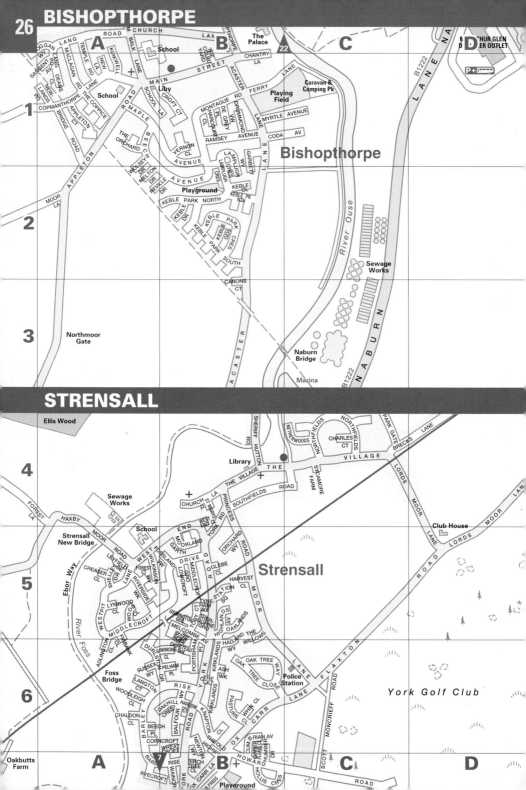

The Index includes some names for which there is insufficient space on the maps. These names are indicated by an * and are followed by the nearest adjoining thoroughfare.

Lerecroft Rd YO24 21 F2
Lesley Av YO10 23 E2
Leven Rd YO24 21 F3
Levisham St YO10 22 D1
Leyfield Cl YO32 26 A5
Leyland Rd YO31 17 F3
Library Sq YO30 4 C2
Lichfield Ct YO23 22 B2
Lidgett Gro YO26 15 E2
Lilac Av YO10 17 G5
Lilac Gro YO32 10 C3
Lilbourne Dr YO30 10 A6
Lilling Av YO31 11 E6
Lime Av YO31 17 F2
Lime Garth YO30 8 B5
Lime Tree Av YO32 10 C3
Lime Tree Mews YO19 19 H3
Lincoln St YO26 15 H3
Lindale YO24 21 E4
Linden Cl YO32 11 E1
Linden Gro YO30 9 H6
Lindley Rd YO30 9 H5
Lindley St YO30 15 H5
Lindley Wood Gro YO30 9 G4
Lindsey Av YO26 15 F4
Lingfield Cres YO24 21 G2
Link Av YO30 10 B6
Link Rd YO31 10 D4
Linley Av YO32 7 E3
Linnet Way YO24 21 E3
Linton Rd YO26 8 C5
Linton St YO26 15 G4
Lister Way YO30 16 A1
Little Av YO30 10 B6
Little Hallfield Rd YO31 5 H2
Little La YO32 6 D3
Little Meadows YO32 6 C4
Little Shambles YO1 5 E3
Little Stonegate YO1 4 D3
Littlefield Cl YO26 8 B4
Littlegarth YO32 6 B4
Livingstone St YO26 15 H3
Lloyd YO31 23 H1
Lochrin Pl YO26 14 D4
Lockey Cl YO24 6 B4
Lockhouse La YO32 7 E4
Lockwood St YO31 5 F1
Lockyer YO30 10 A6
Long Close La YO10 5 F5
Long Furrow YO32 6 C4
Long Ridge Dr YO26 8 C5
Long Ridge La YO26 8 B6
Longcroft YO32 6 B2
Longfield Ter YO30 4 B2
Longwood Link YO30 9 G4
Longwood Rd YO30 9 G4
Lord Mayors Walk YO31 4 D1
Lords Moor La YO32 26 C4
Loriners Dr YO23 24 E2
Lorne St YO23 22 B2
Lorrenger La YO23 20 B3
Love La, Fulford YO10 22 C2
Lovell St YO23 16 C6
Low Fields Dr YO24 15 E6
Low Grn YO23 24 D2
Low La YO10 23 H2
Low Mill Cl YO10 18 A6
Low Moor Av YO10 23 E3
Low Ouse Gate YO1 4 D4
Low Petergate YO1 4 D2
Low Poppleton La YO26 14 D2
Low Westfield Rd YO23 24 B3
Lowcroft YO32 26 B5
Lower Darnborough St YO23 16 C6
Lower Ebor St YO23 16 C6
Lower Friargate YO1 4 D4
Lower Priory St YO1 4 C5
Loweswater Rd YO30 9 G5
Lowfield Dr YO30 6 D2
Lowfield La YO14 14 C4
Lowick YO24 21 E3
Lown Hill YO24 15 E6
Lowther Ct YO31 16 D2
Lowther St YO31 16 C2
Lowther Ter YO24 4 A5
Loxley Cl YO30 9 H4
Lucas Av YO30 16 B1
Lucombe Way YO10 10 C2
Lumley Rd YO30 16 B2
Lund Cl YO32 6 B4
Lunds St YO1 5 E3
Lundy Cl YO10 10 A6
Lycett Rd YO24 21 H4
Lydham Cl YO24 21 E2
Lyndale Av YO10 18 A5
Lynden Way YO24 15 F5
Lynwood Av YO23 24 C2

Lynwood Cl YO32 26 A5
Lynwood Vw YO23 24 C2
Lysander Cl YO30 10 A4
Maclagan Rd YO23 21 H6
Magnolia Gro YO32 10 C4
Maida Gro YO10 22 D1
Main Av YO31 17 E3
Main St, Askham Bryan YO23 20 A5
Main St, Bishopthorpe YO23 26 A1
Main St, Copmanthorpe YO23 24 D3
Main St, Fulford YO10 22 D3
Main St, Heslington YO10 23 G1
Main St, Poppleton YO26 8 B4
Malbys Gro YO23 24 D2
Malham Gro YO31 17 G4
Mallard Way YO32 7 E3
Mallory Cl YO32 10 C2
Malt Shovel Ct YO1 5 E4
Malton Av YO31 17 E2
Malton Rd YO31 17 E2
Malton Way YO30 15 H1
Malvern Av YO26 15 F4
Malvern Cl YO32 11 F1
Mancroft YO32 6 C5
Manley Cl YO32 10 D2
Manor Cl YO26 8 B6
Manor Ct YO32 11 E1
Manor Dr YO19 19 G3
Manor Dr North YO26 15 H6
Manor Dr South YO26 15 H6
Manor Farm Cl YO23 24 C2
Manor Garth YO32 6 B4
Manor Heath YO23 24 C1
Manor La YO30 9 F4
Manor Park Cl YO30 9 G5
Manor Park Gro YO30 9 F4
Manor Park Rd YO30 9 F4
Manor Rd LS24 25 D1
Manor Way YO30 9 G4
Mansfield St YO31 5 F2
Manthorpe Walk YO26 15 G4
Maple Av YO23 26 A1
Maple Ct YO32 10 D3
Maple Gro YO10 22 C2
Maplehurst Av YO31 16 C2
Maplewood Pad YO24 21 E2
March St YO31 16 C3
Margaret Philipson Ct YO10 5 E2
Margaret St YO10 5 F5
Marjorie Waite Ct*, Water La YO30 16 A2
Market St YO1 4 D4
Markham Cres YO31 16 C2
Markham St YO31 16 C2
Marlborough Av LS24 25 A3
Marlborough Dr LS24 25 A3
Marlborough Gro YO10 16 C6
Marmiam Dr YO32 12 D3
Marsden Pk YO30 10 A4
Marston Av YO26 14 D5
Marston Cres YO26 14 D5
Marten Cl YO30 10 A6
Martin Cheeseman Ct YO24 21 E2
Martins Ct YO26 15 H4
Marygate YO30 4 B2
Marygate La YO30 4 B2
Matmer Ct YO10 17 F5
Mattison Way YO24 15 G6
Mayfield Gro YO24 21 G2
Mayfield Ter LS24 25 D1
Maythorn Rd YO31 11 E5
McArthur Glen Designer Outle YO19 22 C6
McHugh Ct YO10 23 G2
Meadlands YO31 17 G3
Meadow Ct, Middlethorpe YO23 22 B5
Meadow Ct, York YO24 21 G2
Meadow Garth LS24 25 D1
Meadow La YO32 6 C4
Meadow Rise LS24 25 D1
Meadow Walk LS24 25 D1
Meadow Way, Huntington YO32 11 F2
Meadow Way, Tadcaster LS24 25 D1
Meadow Way, York YO24 17 F1

Meadowbeck Cl YO10 17 G4
Meadowfields Dr YO31 10 D5
Meam Cl YO10 18 A5
Medway Ho*, Albert St YO10 5 F5
Melander Cl YO26 14 D4
Melander Gdns YO26 6 C5
Melbourne St YO10 16 D6
Melcombe Av YO32 26 B5
Melrose Cl YO31 17 F3
Melrosegate YO31 17 F3
Melton Av YO30 9 H6
Melton Dr, Bishopthorpe YO23 26 A2
Melton Dr, York YO30 9 H6
Melwood Gro YO26 14 D3
Mendip Cl YO32 11 F1
Merchant Gate YO1 5 E4
Merchant Way YO23 24 D1
Merlin Covert YO32 11 E4
Metcalfe La YO19 17 H3
Meworth Mews YO31 5 H1
Micklegate YO1 4 B5
Middle Banks YO32 6 B4
Middlecroft Dr YO32 26 A5
Middlecroft Gro YO32 26 B5
Middleham Av YO31 11 E6
Middlethorpe Cotts YO23 22 B4
Middlethorpe Ct YO23 22 B5
Middlethorpe Dr YO24 21 G4
Middlethorpe Gro YO24 21 G4
Middleton Rd YO24 15 E6
Midway Av YO26 8 C5
Mildred Gro YO24 15 H6
Milford Way YO32 6 D5
Mill Hill Dr YO32 11 E3
Mill La, Copmanthorpe YO23 24 B1
Mill La, Tadcaster LS24 25 C1
Mill La, Wigginton YO32 6 A3
Mill La, York YO31 17 E3
Mill Mount YO24 4 A6
Mill Mt YO24 4 A6
Mill St YO1 5 F5
Millennium Ct YO31 5 H2
Millers Ct YO30 24 D1
Millers Yd YO31 4 D1
Millfield Av YO10 17 F5
Millfield Gdns YO26 8 C5
Millfield La, Poppleton YO26 8 C4
Millfield La, York YO10 17 F5
Millfield Rd YO31 16 B6
Millgates YO26 15 E2
Milner St YO24 15 F5
Milson Gro YO10 17 F5
Milton Carr YO30 9 H6
Milton St YO10 17 F5
Minchin Cl YO30 10 A6
Minster Av YO31 11 E5
Minster Cl YO32 6 C4
Minster Gates YO1 4 D2
Minster Vw YO32 6 C4
Minster Yd, York YO31 4 D1
Minster Yd, York YO1 4 D2
Minter Cl YO32 20 D2
Mistral Ct YO31 16 D1
Mitchell Way YO30 9 G3
Mitchels La YO10 23 F2
Miterdale YO24 21 E4
Moat Fld YO10 17 H4
Moatside Ct YO10 4 C3
Moins Ct YO10 18 A5
Moiser Cl YO32 10 C3
Monk Av YO31 17 E1
Monk Bar Ct YO1 5 E2
Monkgate YO31 5 E1
Monkgate Cloisters YO31 5 F1
Monkgate Ct*, Park Cres YO31 16 D3
Monks Cross Dr YO32 11 G3
Monks Cross Link YO32 11 G1
Monks Cross Shopping Pk YO32 11 G2
Monkton Rd YO31 11 E6
Montague Rd YO23 26 B1
Montague St YO23 22 B2
Montague Walk YO26 8 B5
Montrose Av YO31 16 D1
Moor Gro YO30 21 G2
Moor La, Bishopthorpe YO23 26 A2
Moor La, Copmanthorpe YO23 24 C4
Moor La, Haxby YO32 6 C2

Moor La, Knapton YO26 14 A3
Moor La, Murton YO19 18 C1
Moor La, Strensall YO32 26 B5
Moor La, Towthorpe YO32 7 G4
Moor La, York YO24 20 C4
Moor Lea Av YO24 21 G2
Moor Way YO32 11 F2
Moorcroft Rd YO24 21 F4
Moore Av YO10 17 G4
Moorgarth Av YO24 15 H6
Moorgate YO24 15 F6
Moorland Garth YO32 26 B5
Moorland Gdns YO23 24 D3
Moorland YO10 22 D2
Moorlands Cl YO10 17 H4
Moorlands Fld YO10 23 E2
Moorlands Rd YO30 9 E1
Morehall Cl YO30 9 H4
Morrell Cl YO32 21 E2
Morrell Way YO10 17 G6
Morrill Yd YO1 5 E3
Morritt Cl YO32 11 E6
Moss St YO23 4 B6
Mount Ephraim YO24 4 A5
Mount Par YO24 4 A6
Mount Vale YO24 16 A6
Mount Vale Dr YO24 15 H6
Mowbray Dr YO26 15 E4
Muirfield Way YO26 14 D4
Mulberry Cl YO32 7 E6
Mulberry Dr YO32 6 C2
Mulwith Cl YO31 17 F2
Muncastergate YO31 17 E1
Murray St YO24 15 G5
Murrough Wilson Pl YO31 16 C1
Murton Garth YO19 18 C2
Murton La YO19 18 C2
Murton Way YO19 18 A4
Museum St YO1 4 C3
Myrtle Av YO32 26 B1
Naburn La YO19 22 C6
Nairn Cl YO24 21 E4
Nalton Cl YO23 24 D3
Narrow La YO32 6 A1
Navigation Rd YO1 5 G4
Nelson Ct YO24 21 H2
Nelson St YO31 21 H2
Nelsons La YO24 21 H2
Nessgate YO1 4 D4
Nether Way YO26 8 B5
Netherwindings YO32 7 E3
Netherwoods YO32 26 C4
Neville Dr YO31 16 C2
Neville St YO31 16 C2
Neville Ter YO31 16 C2
Nevinson Gro YO10 23 E3
Nevis Way YO24 20 D4
New Forge Ct YO32 7 E3
New La, Bishopthorpe YO23 26 A1
New La, Huntington YO32 11 F4
New La, York YO24 15 G6
New St, Tadcaster LS24 25 C2
New St, York YO1 4 D3
New Walk YO10 22 C1
New Walk Ter YO10 16 D6
Newborough St YO30 16 B2
Newbury Av YO24 21 F1
Newdale YO32 7 E2
Newgate YO1 5 E3
Newington Ct YO24 21 H1
Newland Park Cl YO10 17 F4
Newland Park Dr YO10 17 F4
Newlands Dr YO26 15 E2
Newlands Rd YO23 26 A1
Newton Ter YO1 4 C6
Newton Way YO32 26 B6
Nicholas Gdns YO10 17 E5
Nicholas St YO10 17 E5
Nidd Cl YO26 8 D6
Nidd Gro YO24 21 G3
Nigel Gro YO24 15 H6
Nightingale Cl YO26 11 E5
Ninth Av YO31 17 F3
Norfolk St YO23 22 B1
Norman Dr YO26 14 D3
Norman St YO10 17 F5
North Easton Ter YO24 21 G2
North Field La YO23 20 A4
North La, Haxby YO32 6 C3
North La, Huntington YO32 11 F1
North La, York YO24 21 F2
North Moor YO32 11 F2

North Moor Gdns YO32 11 F2
North Moor Rd YO32 11 F1
North Par YO30 4 B1
North St YO1 4 C3
North York Trading Est YO30 10 A3
Northcote Av YO24 15 G6
Northcroft YO32 7 E3
Northfield La YO23 14 C3
Northfield Ter YO24 21 G2
Northfields YO32 26 C4
Northlands YO32 7 F5
Northminster Bsns Pk YO26 14 B2
Norway Dr YO10 22 C2
Nunmill St YO23 16 B6
Nunnery La YO23 4 B5
Nunthorpe Av YO23 16 B6
Nunthorpe Cres YO23 22 B1
Nunthorpe Gdns YO23 22 B1
Nunthorpe Gro YO23 22 B1
Nunthorpe Rd YO23 4 B6
Nunthorpe Vw YO23 22 B1
Nursery Cl YO26 8 C5
Nursery Dr YO24 15 G6
Nursery Gdns YO10 17 H5
Nursery Rd YO26 8 C5
Oak Glade YO32 11 E4
Oak Rise YO32 15 E5
Oak St YO26 15 G4
Oak Tree Cl YO32 26 B6
Oak Tree Gro YO32 10 C4
Oak Tree La YO32 6 C5
Oak Tree Way YO32 26 B6
Oakdale Rd YO30 9 H4
Oaken Gro YO32 6 C2
Oakhill Cres YO32 26 B6
Oakland Av YO31 17 F2
Oakland Dr YO31 17 F2
Oaklands YO32 26 B5
Oakville St YO31 16 D1
Ogleforth YO1 5 E2
Old Brewery Gdns LS24 25 D1
Old Coppice YO32 7 E3
Old Dike Lands YO32 6 B5
Old Malton Rd YO32 12 A3
Old Moor La YO24 21 G4
Old Orch YO32 6 D6
Old School Cl YO30 17 G5
Old School Cl YO26 8 B5
Oldman Ct YO24 21 E2
Olympian Ct YO31 17 E5
Orchard Cl YO24 21 G2
Orchard Gdns YO31 11 E4
Orchard Pad YO32 6 D4
Orchard Rd YO26 8 B5
Orchard Vw YO32 8 D1
Orchard Way, Strensall YO32 26 B5
Orchard Way, York YO24 21 G2
Ordnance La YO10 22 D1
Oriel Gro YO10 10 A6
Orrin Cl YO24 21 E4
Osbaldwick La YO10 17 G5
Osbaldwick Link Rd YO19 18 A4
Osbaldwick Village YO10 17 H4
Osborne Dr YO30 9 G3
Osmington Gdns YO32 26 B5
Osprey Cl YO24 20 D3
Ostlers Cl YO23 24 E2
Ostman Rd YO26 15 E3
Otterwood Bank YO24 20 D2
Otterwood La YO24 20 D2
Ouse Acres YO26 15 F3
Ouse Lea YO30 15 H1
Ouse Moor La YO24 8 A4
Ouseburn Av YO26 15 F3
Ousecliffe Gdns YO30 15 H2
Ouston Cl LS24 25 D2
Ouston La LS24 25 D2
Outgang La YO19 18 A4
Overdale Cl YO24 21 F3
Overton Rd YO30 9 F2
Ovington Cres YO23 22 B1
Ovington Ter YO23 22 B1
Owlwood Cl YO19 19 G3
Owlwood La YO19 19 G3
Owston Av YO10 17 F5
Ox Carr La YO32 26 B6
Oxcalder Cl YO19 19 H3

Oxford St YO24 4 A6
Oxton Dr LS24 25 D2
Oxton La LS24 25 D1

Paddock Cl YO23 24 D3
Paddock Way YO26 15 E2
Palmer La YO1 5 F3
Panman La YO19 13 H6
Parade Ct YO31 17 E2
Paragon St YO10 5 F6
Park Av YO32 10 C2
Park Cl YO30 9 E2
Park Cres YO31 16 D3
Park Ct YO31 17 F3
Park Gate YO32 26 C4
Park Gro YO31 16 D2
Park La YO24 15 H5
Park Lodge YO32 10 D2
Park St YO24 4 A6
Parker Av YO26 14 D6
Parkland Dr LS24 25 D1
Parkland Way YO32 6 C4
Parkside Cl YO24 15 G5
Parliament St YO1 4 D3
Pasture Cl, Skelton YO30 9 E1
Pasture Cl, Strensall YO32 26 B6
Pasture Farm Cl YO10 22 D4
Pasture La YO31 11 G6
Pately Pl YO26 15 F5
Patrick Pool YO1 5 E3
Patterdale Dr YO30 9 G5
Pavement YO1 5 E4
Paver La YO1 5 F4
Pear Tree Av YO26 8 C5
Pear Tree Cl YO32 11 F2
Pear Tree Ct YO1 5 F2
Peartree La YO19 19 F3
Peasholme Grn YO1 5 F3
Peckitt St YO1 4 D5
Peel Cl YO10 23 G2
Peel St YO1 5 F5
Pegg La LS24 25 C2
Pelham Pl YO32 26 B6
Pembroke St YO30 16 B2
Penleys Grove St YO31 16 C3
Pennine Cl YO32 11 E3
Penny Lane Ct YO1 5 E2
Pentire Cl YO30 10 A5
Pentland Dr YO32 11 E3
Penyghent Av YO31 17 G3
Peppercorn Cl YO26 15 G4
Peppermill Ct YO31 16 C2
Percys La YO1 5 F4
Peter Hill Dr YO30 16 A1
Peter La YO1 4 D4
Petercroft Cl YO19 19 G2
Petercroft La YO19 19 H2
Petersway YO30 16 A2
Pheasant Dr YO24 20 D3
Philadelphia Ter YO23 22 A1
Phoenix Blvd YO26 15 H4
Piccadilly YO1 5 E4
Pike Hills Mt YO23 24 C1
Piker Thorn La YO19 12 D5
Pilgrim St YO31 16 C2
Pincent Ct YO31 16 D1
Pinders Ct YO1 4 D2
Pinelands YO32 6 C5
Pinelands Way YO10 18 A5
Pinewood Gro YO31 11 E5
Pinewood Hill YO10 18 A6
Pinfold Ct YO30 16 A2
Pioneer Bsns Pk YO30 9 H3
Pit La YO19 19 F3
Plantation Dr YO26 15 E3
Plantation Gro YO26 15 E3
Plantation Way YO32 6 B3
Ploughlands YO32 6 C5
Ploughmans Cl YO23 24 E1
Ploughmans La YO32 6 C5
Plumer Av YO31 17 F4
Pollard Cl YO32 11 E3
Popes Head Alley YO1 4 D4
Poplar Gro YO32 10 D4
Poplar St YO26 15 G3
Poppleton Hall Gdns YO26 8 C4
Poppleton Rd YO26 15 G3
Portal Rd YO26 14 D2
Portisham Pl YO32 26 B6
Portland St YO31 4 D1
Postern Cl YO23 4 D6
Postern Ho YO23 5 E6
Potters Dr YO23 24 E1
Pottery La YO31 16 D1
Powells Yd YO1 5 E2
Precentors Ct YO1 4 D2
Prestwick Ct YO26 14 D4
Prices La YO23 4 C6
Princess Rd YO32 26 B4
Priors Walk YO26 15 F3
Priory Ct YO1 4 C5
Priory St YO1 4 B5
Priory Wood Way YO31 11 E4
Prospect Ct LS24 25 D1
Prospect Dr LS24 25 D1
Prospect Ter, Fulford YO10 22 D4
Prospect Ter, York YO1 4 C5
Pulleyn Dr YO24 21 H1
Pump Ct YO1 5 E3

Quaker Grn YO24 21 E4
Quant Mews YO10 17 G6
Queen Annes Rd YO30 4 B1
Queen St YO24 4 B4
Queen Victoria St YO23 22 A1
Queens Gdns LS24 25 B3
Queens Path YO1 4 D2
Queens Staith Mews YO1 4 D5
Queens Staith Rd YO1 4 D4
Queenswood Gro YO24 15 F6

Railway Ter YO24 16 A5
Railway Vw YO24 21 G2
Rainsborough YO30 10 A6
Ramsay Cl YO31 16 D2
Ramsey Av YO23 26 B1
Ratcliffe Ct YO30 9 E1
Ratcliffe St YO30 16 B1
Raven Gro YO26 15 E4
Rawcliffe Av YO30 9 H6
Rawcliffe Cft YO30 9 F4
Rawcliffe Cl YO30 9 G4
Rawcliffe Dr YO30 9 H6
Rawcliffe Gro YO30 15 H1
Rawcliffe Ind Est YO30 9 G4
Rawcliffe La YO30 9 H6
Rawcliffe Landing YO30 9 E3
Rawcliffe Way YO30 9 F4
Rawdon Av YO10 17 E5
Raynard Ct YO24 21 E2
Rectory Gdns YO23 22 B1
Redbarn Dr YO10 18 A5
Redcoat Way YO24 20 D3
Redeness St YO31 5 G2
Redgrave Cl YO31 16 D1
Redman Cl YO10 22 C2
Redmires Cl YO30 9 H5
Redthorn Dr YO31 11 E5
Redwood Dr YO32 6 C3
Regency Mews YO24 21 H3
Regent St YO10 5 H6
Regents Ct YO26 15 H3
Reginald Gro YO23 22 B2
Reighton Av YO30 9 H6
Reighton Dr YO30 9 H5
Renshaw Gdns YO26 15 G4
Reygate Gro YO23 24 D2
Ribstone Gro YO31 17 G3
Richardson St YO23 16 B6
Richmond St YO31 5 H2
Ridgeway YO26 14 D6
Ringstone Rd YO30 9 H3
Ripley Gro YO32 6 C2
Rishworth Gro YO30 9 H5
Rivelin Way YO30 9 G4
River St YO23 5 E6
Riversdale YO32 7 E3
Riverside Cres YO32 7 E6
Riverside Gdns YO26 8 B4
Riverside Walk, Poppleton YO26 8 B4
Riverside Walk, Strensall YO32 26 A5
Riverside Walk, York YO1 4 C3
Riversvale Dr YO26 8 B4
Robin Gro YO24 15 H6
Robin Hood Yd LS24 25 C2
Robinson Ct YO1 5 F5
Robinson Dr YO24 20 D1
Roche Av YO31 10 D6
Rockingham Av YO31 17 F4
Rogers Ct YO24 21 E2
Roland Ct YO32 11 E3
Rolston Av YO31 11 E4
Roman Cl LS24 25 D1
Roman Way YO30 10 A4
Rookcliffe Ct LS24 25 D1
Ropers Ct YO23 24 E1
Rose St YO31 16 C1
Rose Tree Gro YO32 10 D2
Roseberry Gro YO30 9 H4
Rosebery St YO26 15 H3
Rosecomb Way YO32 6 D5
Rosecroft Way YO30 9 G6
Rosedale Av YO26 15 E5
Rosedale St YO10 22 D1
Rosemary Ct, Tadcaster LS24 25 C1
Rosemary Ct, York YO1 5 G4
Rosemary Pl YO1 5 G4
Rosemary Row LS24 25 C1
Rosslyn St YO30 16 A2
Rougier St YO1 4 C3
Round Hill Link YO30 9 H4
Rowan Av YO32 10 C3
Rowan Pl YO32 10 C2
Rowleys Ct YO32 7 E5
Rowntree Av YO30 10 B6
Royal Chase YO24 21 G3
Ruby St YO23 22 B1
Rudcarr La YO19 13 F5
Ruddings Cl YO32 6 C4
Runswick Av YO26 14 D5
Russell Dr YO30 9 G6
Russell St YO23 16 B6
Russet Dr YO31 17 H3
Rutland Cl YO23 24 D2
Ryburn Cl YO30 9 H4
Rydal Av YO31 17 G3
Rye Cl YO32 6 C4
Ryecroft Av YO24 21 E3
Ryecroft Cl YO31 11 H6
Ryehill Cl YO32 10 D2
Ryemoor Rd YO32 6 C4
Rylatt Pl YO26 14 D6

Sadberge Ct YO10 17 H5
Saddlers Cl YO23 24 D1
Saddlers Walk YO32 11 F4
Sails Dr YO10 17 G6
St Aelreds Cl YO31 17 F4
St Aidans Ct YO10 22 D3
St Andrewgate YO1 5 E3
St Andrews Ct YO1 5 E3
St Anns Ct YO10 16 D6
St Aubyns Pl YO24 16 A6
St Barnabas Cl YO26 15 H3
St Benedict Rd YO23 4 C6
St Catherines Cl YO30 9 E2
St Catherines Pl YO24 4 A6
St Clements Gro YO23 22 B1
St Crux Pass YO1 5 E3
St Denys Rd YO1 5 F5
St Edwards Cl YO24 21 H3
St Georges Pl YO24 21 H1
St Giles Ct YO31 4 D1
St Giles Rd YO30 8 D1
St Giles Way YO23 24 D2
St Helens Rd YO24 21 G2
St Helens Sq YO1 4 D3
St James Cl YO30 9 G3
St James Ct YO26 15 H3
St James Mt YO24 16 A6
St James Pl YO24 21 F2
St Johns Cres YO31 16 C3
St Johns St YO31 5 E1
St Josephs St LS24 25 C2
St Lawrence Ct YO10 23 G2
St Leonards Pl YO30 4 C2
St Lukes Gro YO30 16 B2
St Margarets Ter YO1 5 G4
St Marks Cl YO1 5 F4
St Marks Gro YO30 9 G4
St Martins La YO1 4 C4
St Marys YO30 4 B1
St Marys Cl, Strensall YO32 26 B4
St Marys Cl, Wigginton YO32 6 C3
St Marys Ct YO24 4 B5
St Marys Gro YO10 17 H5
St Marys La YO30 4 B2
St Marys Mews YO32 6 B3
St Marys Sq YO1 5 E4
St Maurices Rd YO31 5 E2
St Nicholas Cft YO23 20 A5
St Nicholas Cl YO23 24 D1
St Nicholas Cres YO23 24 C1
St Nicholas Pl YO10 17 E5
St Nicholas Rd YO23 24 C1
St Nicholas Way YO32 6 B3
St Olaves Rd YO30 16 B3
St Oswalds Rd YO10 22 C3
St Pauls Mews YO24 16 A5
St Pauls Sq YO24 15 H5
St Pauls Ter YO24 16 A5
St Peters Cl YO26 14 C4
St Peters Gro YO30 16 B2
St Philips Gro YO30 16 A1
St Sampsons Sq YO1 4 D3
St Saviourgate YO1 5 E3
St Saviours Pl YO1 5 F3
St Stephens Rd YO24 21 E1
St Stephens Sq YO24 21 E1
St Swithins Walk YO26 15 G5
St Thomas Pl YO31 16 C2
St Thomas's Cl YO10 17 H4
St Wilfrids Rd YO32 7 H1
St Wulstan Cl YO31 16 D1
Salisbury Rd YO26 15 G3
Salisbury Ter YO26 15 H3
Salmond Rd YO24 20 D1
Sandacre Ct YO26 15 F3
Sandcroft Cl YO24 21 F2
Sandcroft Rd YO24 21 F2
Sandfield LS24 25 D1
Sandholme YO32 6 D2
Sandmartin Ct YO24 21 F2
Sandown Cl YO24 21 F1
Sandringham Cl YO32 6 C6
Sandringham St YO10 16 C6
Sandstock Rd YO31 17 G1
Sandygap YO32 6 C5
Sandyland YO32 6 C3
Sandyridge YO26 8 C5
Sargent Av YO23 26 A1
Saville Gro YO30 10 A6
Sawyers Cres YO23 24 E2
Sawyers Walk YO19 19 H2
Saxford Way YO32 6 B3
Saxon Pl YO31 16 D2
Scafell Cl YO30 9 G5
Scaife Gdns YO31 16 C2
Scaife Mews YO31 16 C2
Scaife St YO31 16 C2
Scarborough Ter YO30 16 B2
Scarcroft Hill YO24 16 A6
Scarcroft La YO23 4 B6
Scarcroft Rd YO23,24 4 A6
Scaudercroft YO19 19 H3
Scawton Av YO31 11 E4
School Cl YO30 9 E1
School La, Bishopthorpe YO23 26 A1
School La, Copmanthorpe YO23 24 C2
School La, Dunnington YO19 19 G3
School La, Fulford YO10 22 D3
School La, Heslington YO10 23 G1
School La, Poppleton YO26 8 B5
School St YO24 15 F5
Scott St YO23 16 B6
Scriven Gro YO32 6 D3
Scrope Av YO31 5 H1
Seafire Cl YO30 10 A3
Seaton Cl YO10 17 H5
Second Av YO31 17 E3
Sedge Rise LS24 25 A3
Sefton Av YO31 11 E6
Segrave Walk YO26 15 G4
Selby Rd YO10 22 D4
Seldon Rd YO26 15 G4
Seventh Av YO31 17 E3
Severn Grn YO26 9 E6
Severus Av YO26 15 F4
Severus St YO24 15 F5
Seymour Gro YO31 17 E2
Shallowdale Gro YO10 17 H5
Shannon Ho*, Albert St YO10 5 F5
Shaws Ter YO24 4 B6
Shelley Dr YO32 26 A5
Shelley Gro YO30 9 G6
Sherborne Gro YO32 26 B5
Sheriff Hutton Rd YO32 26 B4
Sherringham Dr YO24 21 F2
Sherwood Gro, Acomb YO26 14 D3
Sherwood Gro, York YO31 11 E5
Shilton Garth Cl YO32 7 F6
Shipton Rd YO30 8 D1
Shipton St YO30 16 B2
Shirley Av YO26 15 E3
Shotel Cl YO30 9 H6
Silver St YO1 4 D3
Silverdale Ct YO24 21 F3
Sim Balk La YO23 21 G5
Simmons Cl YO32 26 A6
Sirocco Ct YO31 16 D1
Sitwell Gro YO26 15 E3
Siward St YO10 17 F5
Siwards Way YO10 17 F6
Sixth Av YO31 17 E3
Skeldergate YO1 4 D4
Skelton Ct YO30 16 A2
Skewsby Gro YO31 11 E5
Skiddaw YO24 21 E3
Slessor Rd YO24 20 D2
Slingsby Gro YO24 21 G3
Smales St YO1 4 C5
Smary La YO19 18 D3
Smeaton Gro YO26 15 E4
Smith Cl YO10 23 E2
Smithie Cl YO32 10 C2
Somerset Cl YO30 9 G4
Somerset Rd YO31 16 D1
South Bank Av YO23 22 B1
South Down Rd YO32 11 F1
South Esp YO1 4 D5
South La YO32 6 C3
South Par YO24 4 B5
South View Ter YO24 15 E5
Southfield Cres YO24 21 G2
Southfields Rd YO32 26 B4
Southholme Dr YO30 9 G6
Southlands YO32 6 C2
Southlands Rd YO23 16 B6
Sowerby Rd YO26 15 F4
Spalding Av YO30 16 A1
Speculation St YO1 5 G5
Spen La YO1 5 E3
Spencer St YO23 4 D6
Spey Bank YO24 21 E4
Spindle Cl YO24 21 E3
Spring Bank Av YO19 19 G2
Spring La YO10 23 G1
Springfield Cl YO31 17 H1
Springfield Ct YO24 15 H5
Springfield Rd YO26 8 B4
Springfield Way YO31 17 G1
Springhill Ct LS24 25 D2
Springwood YO32 6 C5
Spruce Cl YO32 10 C4
Spurr Ct YO24 21 E2
Spurriergate YO1 4 D4
Stabler Cl YO32 6 A3
Stablers Walk YO32 7 E6
Staindale Cl YO30 9 G5
Staithes Cl YO26 15 E5
Stakers Orch YO23 24 D2
Stamford Bridge Rd YO19 18 D4
Stamford St East YO26 15 H3
Stamford St West YO26 15 G3
Stanley Av YO32 6 C6
Stanley St YO31 16 C2
Starkey Cres YO31 17 F4
Station Av YO32 10 D3
Station Ind Est LS24 25 B2
Station Rd, Copmanthorpe YO23 24 D3
Station Rd, Haxby YO32 6 D3
Station Rd, Poppleton YO26 8 B6
Station Rd, Tadcaster LS24 25 B2
Station Rd, York YO1 4 B4
Station Rise YO1 4 B3
Station Sq YO32 26 B5
Steeple Cl YO32 6 A3
Stephenson Cl YO32 11 E5
Stephenson Way YO26 15 H3
Sterne Av YO31 17 F4
Stirling Gro YO10 23 E3
Stirling Rd YO30 9 H3
Stirrup Cl YO24 20 D2
Stockhill Cl YO19 19 G2
Stockholm Cl YO10 22 C2
Stockton La YO31,32 17 E2
Stone Riggs YO32 12 D2
Stonegate YO1 4 D3
Stonegate Arc YO1 4 D2
Stonelands Ct YO30 9 H6
Stones Cl YO24 15 G6
Stonethwaite YO24 21 E4
Stoop Cl YO32 6 B4
Stow Ct YO32 11 E3
Straight La YO19 13 H6
Strakers Pass YO1 5 E4
Stratford Way YO32 11 E3
Stray Garth YO31 17 E1
Stray Rd YO31 17 G2
Straylands Gro YO31 17 E1
Strensall Pk YO32 7 G2
Strensall Rd YO32 7 F6
Stripe La YO30 8 D2
Stuart Rd YO24 15 F6
Stubden Gro YO30 9 H4
Sturdee Gro YO31 16 D1
Stutton Rd LS24 25 B4
Summerfield Rd YO24 21 E3
Sunningdale Cl YO26 14 D3
Sunnydale YO32 6 C5
Surrey Way YO30 9 H6

Surtees St YO30 16 B1
Sussex Cl YO10 17 H6
Sussex Rd YO10 17 H6
Sussex Way YO32 26 A6
Sutherland St YO23 22 B1
Sutor Cl YO23 24 D1
Sutton Way YO30 10 B6
Swale Av YO23 21 G3
Swann St YO23 4 C6
Swarthdale YO32 6 D2
Swinegate YO1 4 D3
Swinerton Av YO26 15 H3
Swinsty Ct YO30 9 H5
Sycamore Av YO32 10 D3
Sycamore Cl, Haxby YO30 6 C5
Sycamore Cl, Skelton YO30 9 E2
Sycamore Fm YO32 26 C4
Sycamore Pl, New Earswick YO32 10 D3
Sycamore Pl, York YO30 4 B1
Sycamore Ter YO30 4 A2
Sycamore Vw YO26 8 B6

Tadcaster Rd YO30 21 E6
Tamworth Rd YO30 10 A6
Tang Hall La YO31 17 F3
Tanner Row YO1 4 C4
Tanner St YO1 4 C3
Tanners Moat YO1 4 C3
Tarbert Cres YO24 20 D4
Tatton Cl YO30 10 A5
Taylors Cl YO19 13 H5
Teal Dr YO24 21 E3
Teck St YO23 16 C6
Tedder Rd YO24 20 D1
Telford Ter YO24 16 A6
Temple Av YO10 17 G4
Temple Garth YO23 24 F3
Temple La YO23 24 D3
Temple Rd YO23 21 H6
Templemead YO31 17 E1
Ten Thorn La YO26 14 C4
Tennent Rd YO24 15 E6
Tennyson Av YO30 16 B1
Terry Av YO23 5 G6
Terry St YO23 22 C1
Thames Ho*, Albert YO24 5 F5
Thanet Rd YO24 21 F2
Thatchers Cft YO23 24 E2
The Avenue, Haxby YO32 6 D4
The Avenue, Southlands YO32 6 C2
The Avenue, York YO30 16 A2
The Beeches YO30 9 E2
The Chestnuts YO32 6 C4
The Close YO30 19 G3
The Copper Beeches YO19 19 G3
The Coppice YO23 26 A1
The Courtyard YO23 22 A6
The Covert YO24 21 H3
The Crescent, Heslington YO10 23 H1
The Crescent, York YO24 4 B5
The Croft YO23 26 B6
The Crossway YO31 17 E1
The Dell YO30 8 D1
The Elms YO32 13 E2
The Esplanade YO30 4 A2
The Fairway LS24 25 B4
The Gallops YO23 20 D3
The Garlands YO30 9 H6
The Glade YO31 17 G1
The Green, Acomb YO26 15 E5
The Green, Dunnington YO19 19 H3
The Green, Skelton YO30 8 D1
The Greenway YO32 6 C5
The Grove YO23 21 G5
The Horseshoe YO24 21 G3
The Knoll YO24 20 D1
The Landings YO32 7 E4
The Leyes YO32 17 H5
The Limes YO24 12 D2
The Link, Copmanthorpe YO23 24 C1

The Link, Fulford YO10 23 E2
The Links LS24 25 B3
The Manor Beeches YO19 19 G3
The Meadows YO30 8 D1
The Mount YO24 4 A6
The Old Highway YO32 26 B6
The Old Orch YO10 22 D4
The Old Village YO32 11 E1
The Orchard, Bishopthorpe YO23 26 A1
The Orchard, Heslington YO10 23 G1
The Paddock YO26 15 E2
The Pastures YO21 21 G2
The Reeves YO24 21 E1
The Ropewalk YO31 5 G2
The Rowans YO32 9 E2
The Shambles YO1 5 E3
The Spinney YO24 21 G4
The Square LS24 25 E1
The Stonebow YO1 5 E3
The Vale YO30 8 D1
The Village, Skelton YO30 8 D1
The Village, Stockton YO32 12 D2
The Village, Strensall YO32 26 B4
The Village, Wigginton YO32 6 B3
The Wandle YO26 14 C6
The Werkdyke YO1 5 F3
The Willows YO32 26 B5
Theresa Cl YO32 11 E6
Thief La YO10 17 E6
Third Av YO31 17 E3
Thirkleby Way YO10 18 A4
Thirlmere Dr YO31 17 G2
Thistleton Ct YO1 5 F5
Thomas St YO10 5 H5
Thompson Pl YO26 15 G4
Thoresby Rd YO24 20 D1
Thorn Nook YO31 17 E1
Thorncroft YO19 19 H3
Thornfield Av YO31 11 E6
Thornfield Dr YO31 11 E5
Thornhills YO32 7 E3
Thornton Moor Cl YO30 9 H4
Thorntree Gro YO30 10 A4
Thornwood Covert YO24 21 E2
Thorpe St YO23 16 B6
Three Cranes La YO1 4 D3
Tilmire Cl YO10 23 E3
Tisbury Rd YO26 15 G4
Tithe Cl YO30 20 D1
Toby Ct YO32 26 B5
Toft Grn YO1 4 B5
Toll Bar Way LS24 25 F1
Tonges St YO1 5 E3
Top La YO23 24 D1
Toremill Cl YO30 10 D2
Torridon Pl YO24 20 D3
Tostig Av YO26 15 E3
Tower Cres LS24 25 B2
Tower Cl YO30 9 H4
Tower Pl YO1 5 E5
Tower St YO1 5 E5
Town End Gdns YO32 6 A3
Townend St YO31 16 C2
Towthorpe Moor La YO32 7 G3
Towthorpe Rd YO26 7 E3
Towton Av YO24 15 H6
Trafalgar St YO23 22 B2
Tranby Av YO10 18 A4
Trenchard Rd YO26 14 D2
Trenfield Ct YO24 15 H5
Trent Av YO24 21 F3
Trent Way YO24 21 F3
Trentholme Dr YO23 16 A6
Trevor Gro YO24 15 H6
Tribune Way YO30 10 A4
Trinity La YO1 4 C4
Trinity Mdws YO32 13 E2
Troon Cl YO26 14 D3
Troutbeck YO24 21 E3
Troutsdale Av YO30 9 G4
Tudor Rd YO24 15 E6
Tuke Av YO10 17 G5
Turbary La YO32 12 A1

Turks Head Ct YO1 5 E2
Turnberry Dr YO26 14 D4
Turners Cft YO10 23 G2
Turnmire Rd YO24 21 G2
Turnpike Rd LS24 25 E1
Twinam Ct YO19 19 H2
Twinpike Way YO32 6 A3
Tyneham Way YO32 26 B5

Ullswater YO24 21 E3
Undercroft YO19 19 H3
Union Ter YO31 16 C3
University Rd YO10 17 F6
Upper Hanover St YO30 15 G3
Upper Newborough St YO30 16 B2
Upper St Pauls Ter YO24 15 H5
Uppercroft YO32 6 C4
Usher La YO32 6 D3
Usher Park Rd YO32 6 D2

Vanbrugh Dr YO10 17 H5
Vanburgh Way YO10 17 H5
Vavasour Ct YO23 24 D3
Vengeance La YO19 19 E2
Vernon Cl YO23 26 B1
Vernon Rd YO30 9 G4
Vesper Walk YO32 7 E6
Vicarage Gdns YO10 11 H6
Vicars Cl YO23 24 D2
Victor St YO1 4 C5
Victoria Cl YO32 15 H3
Victoria St YO23 16 B6
Victoria Way YO32 11 E6
Viking Rd YO26 15 E3
Villa Ct YO26 14 D1
Villa Gro YO31 16 D3
Village Garth YO32 6 B2
Village St, Knapton YO26 14 C3
Village St, Rawcliffe YO30 9 G4
Vincent Way YO24 21 E2
Vine St YO23 16 B6
Vyner St YO31 16 C1

Waggoners Dr YO23 24 E1
Wainers Cl YO23 24 E1
Wains Dr YO24 21 F3
Wains Rd YO24 21 F3
Walker Dr YO24 21 E2
Walmer Carr YO32 6 A3
Walmgate YO1 5 F4
Walney Rd YO31 17 F3
Walnut Cl, Haxby YO32 6 C3
Walnut Cl, Heslington YO10 23 G1
Walpole St YO31 16 C2
Walton Pl YO26 14 D6
Walworth St North YO26 15 H3
Walworth St South YO26 15 H3
Wandhill YO32 6 C4
Wansbeck YO24 20 D4
Warwick St YO31 16 C2
Wasdale Cl YO30 9 G5
Water End YO26 15 G3
Water La, Dunnington YO19 19 H3
Water La, York YO30 10 A4
Waterdale Pk YO31 16 D5
Waterings YO32 6 A3
Waterman Ct YO24 20 D2
Watson St YO24 16 A5
Watson Ter YO24 15 H5
Wattlers Cl YO23 24 E1
Waveney Gro YO30 10 B6
Waverley St YO31 5 E1
Waynefleet Gro YO10 17 G5
Weavers Cl YO23 24 E1
Weddall Cl YO24 21 H2
Welborn Cl YO10 18 A4
Welland Rise YO26 15 F4
Wellesley Cl YO30 10 A5
Wellington Row YO1 4 C3
Wellington St YO10 5 H6
Welton Av YO26 15 F3
Welwyn Dr YO10 22 D2
Wenham Rd YO24 21 E3
Wenlock Ter YO10 22 D1
Wensleydale Dr YO10 18 A4

Wentworth Rd YO24 16 A6
Wentworth Way YO10 23 F1
Wesley Pl YO1 5 E4
West Bank YO24 15 G5
West End YO32 26 A5
West End Cl YO32 26 B4
West Moor Flats YO19 22 D5
West Moor La YO10 23 G2
West Mt LS24 25 B3
West Nooks YO32 7 E3
West Thorpe YO24 21 F2
Westerdale Ct YO30 16 A2
Western Ter YO32 10 D4
Westfield Cl, Poppleton YO26 8 A6
Westfield Cl, Wigginton YO32 6 C3
Westfield Cres LS24 25 B2
Westfield Dr YO10 22 D2
Westfield Gro YO32 6 B3
Westfield La YO32 6 B3
Westfield Pl, Wigginton YO32 6 C3
Westfield Pl, York YO24 20 D1
Westfield Rd YO32 6 C3
Westfield Sq LS24 25 B2
Westfield Ter LS24 25 B2
Westgate LS24 25 C2
Westholme Dr YO30 9 G5
Westlands Gro YO31 17 F1
Westminster Rd YO30 16 A2
Westpit La YO32 26 A5
Westview Cl YO26 14 D2
Westwood Mews YO19 19 H3
Westwood Ter YO23 22 B1
Wetherby Rd, Tadcaster LS24 25 B1
Wetherby Rd, York YO26 14 C5
Wharf Bank Mews LS24 25 C2
Wharfe Dr YO24 21 F3
Wharfedale Cres LS24 25 B2
Wharncliffe Dr YO30 9 H4
Wharton Av YO30 16 B1
Wheatcroft YO32 26 B6
Wheatfield La YO32 6 C4
Wheatlands Gro YO26 15 E3
Wheatley Dr YO32 6 C4
Wheeldale Dr YO32 12 A4
Wheelwright Cl YO24 24 E2
Whenby Gro YO31 11 E5
Whernside Av YO31 17 F3
Whin Cl, Strensall YO32 26 B6
Whin Cl, York YO24 21 H4
Whin Garth YO24 21 H4
Whin Rd YO24 21 H4
Whip Ma Whop Ma Gate YO1 5 E3
Whistler Cl YO23 24 E1
Whitby Av YO31 17 F1
Whitby Dr YO31 17 G2
White Cross Rd YO31 16 C1
White House Dale YO24 21 H1
White House Dr YO24 21 H1
White House Gdns YO24 21 H1
White House Rise YO24 21 H1
White Rose Av YO32 10 C3
White Rose Gro YO32 10 D4
Whitecross Gdns YO31 16 D1
Whitehorse Cl YO32 11 F2
Whitelands YO32 7 F5
Whiteley Cl YO30 10 A5
Whiterose Way YO26 9 E6
Whitestone Dr YO31 10 D4
Whitethorn Cl YO31 11 E4
Whitton Pl YO10 17 H5
Wigginton Rd YO31 16 C1
Wigginton Ter YO31 16 C1
Wighill Garth LS24 25 C1
Wighill La LS24 25 C1
Wilberforce Av YO30 16 B1
Wilkinson Way YO32 26 A5
William Plows Av YO10 17 E6
Willis St YO10 5 G6

Willoughby Way YO24 21 E2
Willow Cft YO26 9 E4
Willow Glade YO32 11 E4
Willow Gro, Earswick YO32 7 F5
Willow Gro, York YO31 17 F3
Willow Rise LS24 25 A3
Willowbank YO10 23 E2
Wilstrope Gro YO10 23 E3
Wilstrope Farm Rd YO23 24 D3
Wilton Rise YO24 15 H5
Wimpole Cl YO30 10 A6
Winchester Av YO26 15 F4
Winchester Gro YO26 15 F4
Windermere YO24 20 D4
Windmill Gro LS24 25 A4
Windmill Ho Ind Est YO23 6 A3
Windmill La YO10 17 G5
Windmill Rise, Tadcaster LS24 25 A4
Windmill Rise, York YO10 15 G5
Windmill Way YO32 6 D3
Windsor Dr YO32 6 A3
Windsor Garth YO24 21 F1
Windsor St YO23 22 A1
Winscar Gro YO30 9 G4
Winterscale St YO10 16 D6
Wisker Dr YO32 7 H4
Witham Dr YO32 11 F1
Wolfe Av YO31 17 F3
Wolsey Dr YO23 26 A2
Wolsley St YO10 5 G6
Wolviston Av YO10 17 H5
Wood Cl YO32 26 A5
Wood St YO31 17 E3
Wood Way YO32 11 F2
Woodcock Cl YO32 7 E3
Woodford Pl YO24 21 F1
Woodhouse Gro YO31 17 G4
Woodland Chase YO30 10 A5
Woodland Way YO32 10 D2
Woodlands YO10 17 G5
Woodlands Av, Tadcaster LS24 25 A3
Woodlands Av, York YO30 6 C4
Woodlands Gro YO31 17 F1
Woodlands Vw LS24 25 A3
Woodlea Bank YO26 15 E4
Woodlea Cres YO26 15 E4
Woodlea Gro YO26 15 F4
Woodleigh Cl YO32 26 A6
Woodside Av YO31 17 F3
Woolnough Av YO10 17 G5
Worcester Dr YO31 17 G3
Wordsworth Cres YO24 21 E3
Wrays Av YO31 10 D6
Wycliffe Av YO10 17 G5
Wydale Rd YO10 18 A4
Wyre Ct YO32 6 C3
Wyre Mews YO32 6 C3

Yarburgh Way YO10 17 H5
Yearsley Cres YO31 16 D1
Yearsley Gro YO31 11 E5
Yew Tree Mews YO10 17 H4
York Bsns Pk YO26 9 E6
York Rd, Acomb YO26 15 E5
York Rd, Dunnington YO19 19 H3
York Rd, Haxby YO32 6 D6
York Rd, Strensall YO32 26 B6
York Rd, Tadcaster LS24 25 D1
York St YO23 19 G3
Yorkfield La YO23 24 E1
Younger Ct YO10 23 G2